Made in the USA
Monee, IL
07 March 2023

29379841R00057